blue
rider
press

I WANT to KILL the DOG

I WANT to KILL the DOG

RICHARD M. COHEN

BLUE RIDER PRESS

a member of Penguin Group (USA) Inc.

New York

Adios, Jasper.

53702478

636.70092
COH

blue
rider
press

Published by the Penguin Group
Penguin Group (USA) Inc., 375 Hudson Street, New York, New York 10014, USA •
Penguin Group (Canada), 90 Eglinton Avenue East, Suite 700, Toronto,
Ontario M4P 2Y3, Canada (a division of Pearson Penguin Canada Inc.) •
Penguin Books Ltd, 80 Strand, London WC2R 0RL, England • Penguin Ireland,
25 St Stephen's Green, Dublin 2, Ireland (a division of Penguin
Books Ltd) • Penguin Group (Australia), 707 Collins Street, Melbourne,
Victoria 3008, Australia (a division of Pearson Australia Group Pty Ltd) •
Penguin Books India Pvt Ltd, 11 Community Centre, Panchsheel Park,
New Delhi–110 017, India • Penguin Group (NZ), 67 Apollo Drive,
Rosedale, Auckland 0632, New Zealand (a division of Pearson
New Zealand Ltd) • Penguin Books, Rosebank Office Park, 181 Jan Smuts
Avenue, Parktown North 2193, South Africa • Penguin China, B7 Jaiming Center,
27 East Third Ring Road North, Chaoyang District, Beijing 100020, China

Penguin Books Ltd, Registered Offices: 80 Strand, London WC2R 0RL, England

Photographs on pages 13, 87, 91, and 99 courtesy of Nancy Murray.
Photograph on page 107 courtesy of Philip Friedman/Good Housekeeping.

Library of Congress Cataloging-in-Publication Data

Cohen, Richard M.
I want to kill the dog / by Richard M. Cohen.
p.   cm
ISBN 978-0-399-16203-9
1. Cohen, Richard M.   2. Cohen, Richard M.—Family.   3. Dog owners—United
States—Biography.   4. Dog owners—United States—Psychology.   5. Dogs—Social
aspects—United States.   6. Human-animal relationships—United States.   7. Popular
culture—United States.   I. Title.
SF422.82.C64A3   2012   2012028039
636.7—dc23

Printed in the United States of America
1   3   5   7   9   10   8   6   4   2

This book is printed on acid-free paper. ∞

BOOK DESIGN BY AMANDA DEWEY

ALWAYS LEARNING   PEARSON

With Illustrations

by Stan Mack

This book is dedicated

to numerous individuals,

all of whom declined the honor.

A HAIKU

Domesticated.
Wolf sits by the fire, waiting,
rattlesnake in fur.

Domesticated?
You've got to be kidding.

I WANT to KILL the DOG

"Bye, Jasper

I ask you. Has a couple ever gone to war or a spouse moved to another country because a pet came between them? Have two people other than my wife and me ever had such opposing feelings when it comes to domestic animals?

The irony is that my wife encouraged—no, goaded—me into writing this book about our dog. Make that *her* dog, whom I came to dislike long ago. My good wife must have figured telling my story would calm me down, maybe even shut me up about the beast.

Not a chance.

Jasper is a loud little doggie, with an ear-splitting bark that explodes with clocklike precision. To make matters worse, the animal's personality matches the noise. Jasper can be just plain mean, at least to me. Jasper has an inflated sense of authority that goes unchallenged. I gave up long ago.

My wife is a happy puppy prisoner and unreconstructed animal apologist. The woman lends a beautiful face to a culture that celebrates the pet pedestal, where lazy animals vegetate as owners pop grapes into their always-open mouths. Spare me, please.

I want to tell my story before my betrothed,

a fauna fanatic, gets her version out. There is a context here, a culture overtaking and suffocating me. It is a pet culture, powerful and peculiar. My mate buys in big-time, and she is not alone. Out West, dogs are dogs, tough and terrific, roaming the plains. In New York, maybe in all metropolitan areas, most doggies are wimps, cute, cuddly, and coddled.

In fact, animal coddling is elevated to an art form. In the Big Apple, it is everywhere. There is doggie day care, a booming business serving privileged corporate canine clients that cannot bear to be alone during the day. These beasts luxuriate in splendor. I often spot vehicles marked with "Pet Limousine" signs being met by doormen on Park Avenue. What is wrong with this picture?

A new online service draws a distinction between a dog owner and a dog parent. A dog parent is someone who really, *really* loves their animal. They are people who cannot do enough for da' darling dog. So now there is Bark Box (or Barf Box, as I like to say), an online product full of things like dog-bone-shaped ice cube trays that make dog treats or a dog massager. I think I need a Barf Box.

I believe the pet culture is over the top. Books help define any culture, and America devours loony literature that celebrates mass anthropomorphism by the ton. This goofy animal culture has seized America by the throat.

Doggie lit travels with warp speed from the sublime to the ridiculous. From talking to teaching, reality has no place here. Still, these books frequently land on bestseller lists. Go figure.

This fine literature actually seems to speak to people. Do dogs really have some mystical superhuman power to guide mere mortals through difficult lives? People sure seem to think so.

Take Garth Stein's novel, *The Art of Racing in the Rain*. In fact, take it as far from me as you can. "Enzo knows he is different from other dogs: a philosopher with a nearly human soul." You're kidding. Right?

"He has educated himself by watching television extensively, and by listening very closely to the words of his master, Denny Swift, an up-and-coming race car driver." Stop right there.

Denny cannot be so swift if he drives souped-up cars around in circles and defies death for hours as he works out a teaching plan for his dog. It must be hard to teach a dog to be a person. The book, of course, is one of those runaway bestsellers.

Then there are Cesar Millan's books about training your dog while being its friend. Important stuff. The author shares secrets about improving your relationship with your dog. If you stepped in *that*, you would be cleaning your shoes off for a month.

Don't take my word for it. "Being able to set and communicate boundaries is one of the most important roles that you play as your puppy's pack leader." I am definitely *not* my puppy's pack leader. I am readying my application to be his executioner. And this: "Communication, to me, is first intent, then energy, then body language, and lastly, sound." What is this guy talking about?

And do not overlook *Puppy Diaries: Raising a Dog Named Scout*, an estrogen-drenched animal love story between a golden retriever and the editor of *The New York Times*. So much in common. No staff reviewer is going to scream to Jill Abramson, "Hold the syrup. You're drowning the pancake."

I can assure you, the mutt that lives in my house is ordinary at best, pathological at worst. Let's settle on maladjusted. Jasper flunked philosophy and was kicked out of charm school. And I just can't bring myself to sign the ungrateful animal up for canine corrective camp in the Catskills. Attitude adjustment can be expensive. So is psychotherapy on the East Side of Manhattan.

So I will have to live with our psychotic dog and his screaming, screeching bark. Jasper will continue going for my neck when I go near my lovely lady, who the dopey dog thinks is his trophy wife and, coincidentally, happens to feed him twice a day.

So far, we are surviving, but something has to give.

The following is a true story.

I WANT to KILL the DOG

First of all, Jasper is not my dog, just the family animal, a mutt, to be precise. Jasper is nothing but trouble. But of course, I am the problem. That is how it works in our house. That crazy animal has turned the place upside down, but I usually take the blame for causing chaos and provoking Jasper's chronic bad behavior. I am innocent, I swear.

Jasper belongs to my wife and to the ages, though few will believe my story. And a sad story it is. And noisy. Jasper runs around barking like a maniac, as if his tail is caught in an electric socket. This version of man's best friend is just plain annoying.

It all began the day my wife bought Jasper from a pet store. Who buys animals from pet stores anymore? Poor, sickly, undernourished creatures with smoker's cough arrive at homes from pet stores, animals that are down and out. Maybe they have TB, worms, or whatever. In Jasper's case, it surely was distemper, and it proved contagious. Now I have it, too.

The seedy pet emporium sat across the street from my kids' school, next to Jasper's, a favorite pizza joint. You can guess the rest. The

JASPER PREPARING to WATER.
the PLANTS.

owner of the pet store told my wife Jasper is an Aussie poo. Never give a sucker an even break.

Genetic tests later indicated that Jasper is a dog of many flavors and what is known as a mutt.

The dog's only papers covered the kitchen floor where he slept as a puppy. The poodle palace is gone now. Not so the dog. Meredith claims Gabe, our second kid, predicted that Jasper would return joy to the family. Return joy? Where the hell was happiness hiding?

Gabe denies he ever said such a thing. I reached him at college and he seemed to wonder why I was bothering him with this foolish question. I explained that it was his goofy mother who probably made the whole thing up to head off buyer's remorse. Mine.

WHAT RICHARD SEES

WHAT JASPER SEES

Please allow me to present my opening argument in *Richard M. Cohen v. Jasper, the Hideous Shrieking Pig Dog.* This is an open-and-shut case, and I want damages. Jasper's ear-piercing bark is continual and is disturbing the peace, the animal screaming as if our car is rolling over his private parts, not that they still exist.

Jasper dislikes me as much as I loathe him. The animal bares his teeth and lunges at me whenever I go near my wife. He tries to tear my face off, because the animal is possessive, if not pathological, and believes she is his betrothed. Your Honor, these are only the highlights of my case. Please hear my story.

SCORECARD

My wife is Meredith Vieira, journalist, television star, and fabulous mom. Jasper is simple enough to believe what he sees on television: Meredith sane and serene and fully in control. The problem begins with the fact that my good wife has her moments when she is none of the above. Ms. M. has a few loose screws when it comes to pets and other living things.

Of course, the public thinks Meredith can do no wrong. But when you walk on water, sooner or later you get wet. Right now no jury in the land would give me a fair shake. If Meredith and I stand on opposite sides of an issue, such as a crime against humanity—that would be Jasper—we all know who is going to prison.

The fact that the woman is a fanatic animal person will be held as inadmissible. Besides, no one will believe that she takes orders from our hairy creatures, except people who know the lady has a big heart that overrules her brain.

Meredith routinely chases insects around the house to capture them in a glass or jar to be released in the great outdoors, where no doubt they will be devoured by birds or frogs, which is precisely why the bugs hide indoors in the first

place. Meredith never will step on an ant. Big deal. Neither will I, though I refuse to walk in front of an approaching train to avoid insect carnage.

Our kids just watch in wonder, smiling as they silently roll their eyes. They know their mom pretty well. And they can predict my stunned silence. Their eyes go back and forth between the two of us as they hold their tongues.

I imagine them waving a Swiss flag and declaring their neutrality. Yet it never ceases to amaze the three of them as they witness their mother running around in what should be a Red Cross uniform, jar in hand, yelling to no one in particular, "Open a window. I have to free the poor bug."

Case in point: About two decades ago,

when the kids were young, we had two cats, Spike and Beanbag. Spike had a kidney disease, and we taught Ben, our older son, to give him IV treatments each day. We came home one night to learn that Spike was dying. Ben was maybe halfway through elementary school and needed to be consoled.

What's a mother to do? Actually, I am not certain Mom was up to the assignment. Meredith walked around the house, crying and holding the dead cat in her arms. When I awoke the next day in an empty bed, I ventured into the library to find Meredith asleep in a chair, still holding a rather stiff cat.

I awakened her and suggested she put the cat in the frigid garage. "It's cold out there," she cried. That is the point, dear: the house will smell a little better. These cats were our first animals in the house. I thought my wife would don sackcloth and ashes in mourning.

Meredith hired a band of workers from somewhere in South America to dig a hole in the frozen ground. They dug a grave large enough for an elephant and fled the moment they were done, no doubt believing the resting place was for a person.

Meredith opened the windows and blared out music from *The Lion King*, conducting a funeral exotic enough for Simba to attend. Dr. Dolittle was invited, too. I don't remember if he made it.

I do have confirmation that Meredith and the kids danced around the giant grave and Ben was lowered in, carrying the cat corpse

Spike.
Entering the Petrified Forest.

and notes to the cat's spirit from the three youngsters. I could not get away from the office that afternoon.

It is fair to say all of us are acutely aware that Meredith is an animal acolyte. She tells the story of growing up close to her grandfather's farm near Newport, Rhode Island.

Meredith's grandfather had chickens, a cow and bull, and assorted barnyard animals. And he could not bring himself to slaughter any living thing. By all accounts, he was a very nice man. So he survived by raising and selling strawberries and vegetables.

This gentle farmer also put food on his own table by running a laundry. Feeding animals and feeding animals to people are certainly different ways of looking at farming.

Apparently the man loved having animals too much to lose them.

Meredith visited the farm constantly as she grew up. Her family's cats, Cesar, Cramden, and Norton, plus a few others, all came from her grandpa's barn. Her love of animals is due in large part to his. So Meredith comes by her love of animals honestly.

That does not mean her animal affection is not carried to extremes. Beasts are elevated to ethereal heights, furry spirits on our tiny suburban farm. Meredith certainly likes Jasper, our scraggly pain in the ass, a lot more than she likes me. Who doesn't?

Plenty of our friends have no use for the animal. Yet few want to burst Meredith's bubble. People are tired of the hideous noise, weary of being accosted, teeth flashing, if they are brave enough to kiss Meredith on the cheek when they arrive for a visit. The dog feels a special enmity for guys, which he used to be. That may be because women show patience while their husbands try to kick the wretched animal in the face.

One female friend has the annoying habit of telling me that Jasper is a good boy, even though the dog goes for her ankles whenever she shows up. I have no explanation for this. She is another dog apologist in my life. If I did not like her so much, I would throw her out of the house before dinner. I wish I had a dollar for every person who has whispered, "How can you stand that dog?"

No. I am not envious of my sexy wife's

devotion to Jasper. Nor am I suspicious of it, so don't even go there. I will not allow you to dismiss my feelings as the product of petulance. I do not want to be a dog. I refuse to eat dry food on the floor, and besides, the meals suck.

Plus, I dislike authority figures. Dogs are supposed to serve people, not vice versa. The relationship is called indentured servitude. Jasper seems to take no offense at the fact that Meredith is a slave owner.

And Meredith routinely dismisses my complaints about Jasper. She has heard them one too many times. "Richard hates dogs," she will tell anyone with ears.

I have ears myself and do not hate dogs. I grew up with one. He was a Welsh terrier who met his end under a station wagon, traumatizing the entire family. If you are a shrink, don't even start.

I believe in tolerance for people and pets, a live-and-let-live attitude toward household animals and their wacky owners. The problem is that, in my joint, anything short of unbridled love is up there with war crimes, punishable by . . . you do not want to know.

I like the strong *silent* type. Large, loving beasts are a joy. One deep-throated woof of warning when necessary is enough. Message sent. Our dog is a windup toy, a stuffed animal that runs around in circles, loud and self-absorbed. He has elevated yipping to an art form. Our family has been domesticated and serves him. What is wrong with this picture?

I only want what is best for Jasper. I hope

to set him free from bondage and let him run. And run and run. The animal can send us a postcard when he gets to Des Moines and finds a paying job.

Is it such an unreasonable request that the dog learn to behave and stop bothering everyone? Instead, maybe there is an acceptable way to part company with the animal. An annulment will be fine. No alimony is necessary. No obligations. I wish the old boy no harm. I am a gentle soul.

Well, that is not exactly true. In fact, it is a lie.

I want to kill the dog.

To that end, I have given Jasper options. I asked the dog if he would consent to an operation, specifically, open-heart surgery with a butter knife. (You can't neuter him twice.) It seemed only right to ask for his consent. The dog did not answer. I believe his lawyer counseled him to remain silent.

The animal has pushed me perilously close to the edge. Clearly, I am teetering. I talk to Jasper, out loud and in animated tones. Usually, I insult the dog, saying ugly things about him and his mother in a pleasant enough tone of voice, coaxing him out of the house to put as much distance between us as possible. The door locks. When he peers in through a window, I give him the finger. How sick is that?

I would get some small satisfaction if Jasper could sense my antipathy toward him. Maybe he does get it but says nothing. He generally ignores me when he isn't attacking me, as if he cannot be bothered. I watch him watch me, disinterested and desperately bored, looking for something, anything, to look at as he rests without a thought in his head. Jasper is exhausted from doing nothing.

I have not been shy about describing various options for doing away with the animal. I cannot elaborate here without having to move to another bedroom. My hands are tied, anyway.

If anything untoward, such as, say, murder, were to visit Jasper's kingdom, all fingers would point to me. Even if I were walking on the moon or 20,000 leagues under the sea doing important research when it happened, Meredith would immediately have a warrant for my arrest sworn out. And I would go to the chair while echoes of Jasper were heard in the next county.

A History Lesson

How did this happen to me? What did I do wrong? Job never had it this bad. It's a mystery, because the first step into dogland felt so right. Ben was our only kid then. He loved dogs and threw himself at them unflinchingly. Our family trek through the Wild Kingdom began when the lad was barely two. The year was 1990, and Ben was sucking all the energy out of the house.

The journey of a thousand miles began as Meredith was minding her own business in her office at *60 Minutes*, and a stray dog magically appeared. It had been found wandering in Riverside Park along the Hudson River by a couple of young staffers. The little doggie found his way to Meredith, passed Go, and collected $200, which he did not share. A bad beginning.

Meredith asked me to come over to meet the little puppy, and I knew he had already joined the family. It seems like a long time ago. Ben has finished college and lives in Shanghai now, an indication of how long it has been and how far he has traveled to escape the mammal madness enveloping his homeland.

Adopting a dog was no small deal. A friend in the city had told me dogs are worse than kids. Children have at least a small chance of learning something, anything. Dogs, on the other hand, are and always will be blank slates. But no alarms sounded, no sirens wailed inside my skull.

After all, I did demand naming rights for our first new dog and somehow got them. Willie seemed like the right name for a mutt discovered hanging with hobos by the river. Meredith probably would have gone for something more elegant. "Willie" was a poor man's "Reginald," a fit for a sort of scrappy terrier. Willie was a small dog, though still young. Most importantly, Willie was a boy's dog.

I imagined Ben announcing, "I'm going out to play ball with Willie," and hearing the reassuring sound of the screen door slamming behind him. Our Irish babysitter later informed me that, in her country, Willie is what a guy's private parts are called. I believe that was my last contribution on matters animal, vegetable, or mineral.

Willie and Ben were instant buddies. The system was working. I thought Willie *enriched* our lives. I did. What a splendid, though highly subjective notion. Life in our house would change; that tired expression, *enriching our lives*, would become a phrase used against me with pets to come. Willie seemed an okay pet, at least for a while.

It could not have been six months later when the dog was hit by a car—two cars, actually—and left for a goner. A vet had

Ben with Willie. The Beginning of a bad dream.

doubted poor Willie would make it through the night, but the scrappy animal rallied.

Willie would make it through more nights and burn through many dollars, fifteen thousand of them, to be precise. Later, we knew the dog would survive. I thought all of us would have to move out of our new home and back to Willie's old territory, the more affordable wilds of Riverside Park by the Hudson.

Willie was in bad shape for a long time. At first, the poor dog could barely stand. He quivered and shook when he tried. Meredith left for work every day before I did. My mission was clear. And rather unpleasant. In fact, I could not believe I had become an orderly for the mutt, but I gritted my teeth and did my duty. Each morning, I struggled to lift Willie as if he were a hand-carved, wooden cigar-store dog and deposit him outside before he peed on my hands.

When I picked him back up for the return trip, the walk to the front door was not a fabulous aesthetic experience. My hands were strangely moist. Make that wet. I renamed the dog Willie Wet Cock.

This went on for months. I was doing my part. Willie was slowly improving and began to walk again. The days of compulsively washing my hands with a vengeance before just about any activity finally vanished.

The dog had aged after the accident and now moved like an old man, though eventually he could run pretty fast. Like, away. Whenever possible. Willie would flee the house like an escaping convict. He never came back willingly. The police knew who we were because of Willie, also because a babysitter once started a fire in the oven by heating up a pizza that was still in the box, but that's another story.

I guess I can't totally blame Willie for putting us on the cops' list of high-risk homeowners. But they did keep their eyes on us because of him. The dog fled the premises frequently. When the police found him, a cruiser would show up in our driveway with their buddy Willie sitting up front, riding shotgun like he belonged there. It was cute, at least for a while. I think the cops should have given Willie a badge to wear on his policeman's hat.

By now, we had three children. Gabe and Lily had joined the menagerie. They fit right in, and family chaos was ratcheted up a notch. Most of the time, the house was up for grabs. Willie was in his element but moving into his nuisance phase. I think his aging body was beginning to ache from his collisions with cars years earlier. The dog's temperament took a turn for the worse, too.

Willie took to accosting passing bicyclists, including children. He would nip at their feet. He was scaring friends and neighbors, not to mention passersby, who were ambushed regularly. Grown guys were smart and just kicked at him as hard as they could. Women were more gentle, frequently tumbling onto our front lawn to avoid hitting the animal. Little kids just started crying and instantly fell off their bikes.

The dog went after me occasionally.

Nipping had turned to biting. First it was just the air near a foot, then an ankle. Once, I tried to kick him hard and missed, joining half the neighborhood, the legion of kickers, piled high on the lawn. The milk of human kindness in me was beginning to sour.

I am pretty sure that was the point when I began to question why humans collect pets. "They enrich our lives," Meredith answered. Right. By now I was thinking maybe, just maybe, pets are more trouble than they are worth. Life with Willie had changed.

Then I went from annoyed to pissed. The dog chewed up my souvenirs from years in the news business. When Willie tore up and half devoured a baseball cap reading U.S.S. Something-or-Other, given to me by the captain of a landing craft anchored in Beirut harbor, I went over the edge. I had survived covering a long war in Lebanon and now was fighting my own dog for the spoils. I wished I could locate my dusty old AK-47.

Willie had been with us for about eight years and pretty much had the run of the house. Life must have been too calm. So out of nowhere and with no warning, Meredith adopted Shea.

ENTER the Horse

Suddenly there was another animal in the house claiming to be a dog. Instantly I knew better, but did not know how to react, or even what to think. At first I was fine with it, though mystified by my wife's enthusiasm for throwing a live grenade into the living room.

Shea was a real dog. A big dog. Actually, Shea was a behemoth. Of course, any decision to acquire another animal should have been a family affair. That is how to preserve the peace. Peace was, alas, elusive. No one fought the addition. I knew it would be like talking to my foot.

Shea resembled a small horse, and I began to think maybe he was not a dog at all. He should have been eating hay. Shea was jet-black and all muscle. He could have run the Preakness.

I never knew his breed, but his coat was smooth and this doggie or horsie was as big as the stadium where he turned up. If Meredith was looking for trouble, bingo, she found it. Shea was the heftiest child in the house.

Gabe is and always has been a Mets fan. Meredith heard that a stray had been found hanging around a parking lot at Shea Stadium,

SHEA.
A GIANT PAIN.

the tired old ballpark where the Mets used to play, and decided she had to adopt it for Gabe.

It is possible the woman may have made this move out of misplaced loyalty to Gabe. But clearly she has a taste for chaos and strays, and the two seem to go together. This particular hobo could have crushed the only Mets fan in the house. Little Gabe.

Shea Stadium is where the Mets defeated the Red Sox to win the 1986 World Series. I don't know if the Divine Ms. M. (a Red Sox fan) remembered that we were there for the last game of that memorable series. Meredith is a forgiving person, though, even with me. I am not certain she even thought of the team's history or her second son's love for the team. That series came long before Gabe. As a matter of fact, I have no idea what or if she was thinking when she brought Shea home.

Maybe someone made a bet that Meredith could be conned into adopting the pony. Or somebody dared her. My money is on the fact that my wife cannot complicate life enough. We kept Shea indoors, of course. I did not want to scare the neighbors.

Besides, I lived in fear that Shea would collide with a car. That would have been like a high-speed embrace between a motorcycle and an elephant, clearly not good for the cyclist. Not good for me. Great for the lawyers. Have you ever seen a car after it collided with a moose? Shea would have walked away without a scratch.

None of us knew quite how to relate to

Shea, though our three small children did not seem the slightest bit intimidated. Eventually we let him venture outdoors.

And our rat pack ran around the house and through the yard oblivious to the moose hiding somewhere in the bushes, towering over the foliage, actually. I lived with the fear that sooner or later we would hear a loud belch and there would be only two children running around the house and through the yard.

Willie was not amused. He was getting older by the minute and was semiretired as the neighborhood terrorist. The vet had warned us that, since the poor dog had been welded together after slow dancing with a moving car, he probably would have a shorter life expectancy than normal. Shea seemed determined to make that happen.

Willie would go missing for extended periods, not to be found by anyone, especially Shea. I think the gigantic beast frightened Willie much more than he actually threatened him. Meanwhile, the gentle giant terrorized the house.

I dared to take him for walks, imagining with horror what a supersized mess he would make on the floor if I waited too long, and wanting to avoid the same mess on our lawn. That was not going to happen on my watch. But I did learn the hard way not to walk directly behind Shea.

And I would not let one of our pint-sized

kids walk the giant on four legs. Shea was many times heavier than all of them weighed together. I pictured Lily grabbing the leash and getting dragged to New Jersey.

Chaos was spreading.

Shea often got out of the house as our small troop was gathering to leave for school and work. The twenty-minute ride to school had become a wonderful ritual, a time for family fighting when bonding became boring. Then Shea stepped into the batter's box, and all hell broke loose. The game immediately was sent into extra innings. The car remained in Park for what seemed an interminable period as we tried to recapture the bounding beast.

Shea came right out of *War of the Worlds*, Tom Cruise's movie about alien monsters from space trying to take over. There the extraterrestrial dog was, running around outdoors, larger than life, like the crazy horse he was. Shea was grabbing coats and stealing books, even holding lunches in his teeth, with hats and gloves and assorted items strewn around our property. The yard looked as if a typhoon had blown through.

If the dog saw one of us approaching an item on the lawn, he would drop everything to thunder over and grab it before one of us got there. Screams filled the air. Where were the cops when we needed them? Where was the National Guard?

The kids were not happy. They wanted to get in the car and go and instead were watching a three-hundred-pound fullback steaming down the field and jumping over them. The tears would begin as our children imagined starting the day in the school office with an excuse that sounded an awful lot like "The dog ate my homework." If the kids did not like Shea, they never let on. Maybe they just wanted to please their mother. Children have been driven into therapy for less.

Then Meredith would walk out of the house, and the last kernel of calm was transformed into hysteria. My low-key wife became a maniac, dropping everything, her own books and reams of paper, as she joined the chase.

Meredith never really got angry. She had brought this monster into our lives and was not about to concede remorse. Instead, she started screaming and reasoning with Shea as she followed the dog around the yard. Reasoning with an animal. That always works.

The dog would double back and grab some of her belongings, including research for one of that day's segments of *The View*. The sighs became louder. Cars going by would stop as an audience built. Some impatient commuters would start honking as the wild scene spread to the streets. This became a recurring theme. I think our neighbors were amused.

I hadn't screamed like that since the Beatles came to town. It was great. Surprisingly, it took very little food to calm the moose down, that is, when we could slow him down long enough to offer it. Shea was a cheap date.

Willie, by the way, was nowhere to be seen during all this, cowering deep in my closet, hiding under dirty laundry. This spot was the quivering animal's new home. My thought that this was no way for Beaver Cleaver to live was ripening. I do not know what Wally would have thought about our delightful pets, but my life had been *enriched* enough. We were fast losing our status as the all-American family.

Then, amidst the household's constant uproar, we almost lost Shea. Meredith and I had purchased a basketball hoop for pickup games in the driveway. Filling a modest-sized tank in the base with water stabilized the metal frame. We were shivering through the middle of an especially frigid winter and were advised to mix the water with a healthy dose of antifreeze. *Healthy* may not be exactly the right word.

Antifreeze, it turns out, was an aphrodi-

RICHARD M. COHEN

siac for the moose. *Poison* is another colorful term. We had left an open can of that thick, sweet-smelling stuff lying around outdoors. What did we know? We had no idea it had mystical powers, summoning a dog to its doom. When Shea polished off the rest of the antifreeze, I just figured the animal was down a quart. Meredith managed to remain calm.

But like Willie years before him, our daredevil dog cheated death that cold, cold night. Then, once again, we got the bill. I caught Shea ordering another drink and told him his bar tab was getting out of hand.

By now, these animals were into us for tens of thousands of dollars. This situation was not making sense. Living in misery and paying through the nose for the honor was nothing less than insane, in my mind only, of course. We had been down that road before, but now it seemed unending.

Fortunately, a happy resolution came unexpectedly. The lady from the animal shelter where we had officially adopted Shea made a routine call to ask about the dog's well-being. Meredith said the doggie was fine but drank too much. When we told her Willie tried to kill himself, the old white lie to make the point that our aging mutt was tired of feeling intimidated, she grew self-important and stern.

The woman was humorless. She seemed more concerned about Shea than poor Willie, probably worried that if Shea committed suicide, she might be sentenced to the slammer as an accessory to the crime. I was in Willie's corner, tired of the horse. The lady said not every dog is suited for all homes and announced she was recalling Shea. "But we love him," Meredith pleaded. I thought that was stretching the truth just a little.

"This is not about you," the lady lectured in a voice as warm as cold antifreeze. "Our priority is the welfare of animals, not people." Well, excuse me. And then Shea was gone.

There were no tears at the dinner table, not even from my wife. Nobody hated Shea, but it was time to trade him to another team. Eventually Willie hobbled out of the closet, looking like an old man being released from a home for the aged. Our pal Willie would last a few more years before wasting away, probably from his old injuries. He had redeemed himself during the moose's reign and kept his dignity. The moment was sad for all of us.

The doggie drama was getting old by this point. I had gone through enough with pets and vets. There is a big difference between animals in the abstract and those in your face. In our family, however, anything worth doing is worth overdoing. The question became not *what* but *when*. I intuitively knew it was only a matter of time.

I called Meredith's old friend Priscilla. The two had gone to elementary school together and have stayed close. "Why does Meredith do this stuff?" I asked point-blank. "We are raising three kids, one a young teenager. We work hard. Keep terrible hours. Already we live with stress. Why does she feel the need to complicate everything?"

Priscilla sighed. "Some people feel guilty if life is too easy." Okay. "Meredith probably thrives on chaos." Maybe. "And there are those who think the crazier life is, the more exciting it becomes." Nothing I hadn't thought of.

"In other words, you don't know," I said.

"Right," she replied apologetically.

The Monster from the Black Lagoon

I t is said that good things come in threes. And so do bad things. Never light three cigarettes with one match. Then there were the famous three blind mice, not to mention the Three Stooges. They were our role models.

So along came Samantha, our third dog. Samantha was not an attractive girl. She was plucked from a local shelter less than a year after we lost Shea, who was eventually adopted by some agility dog trainer, whatever that is.

Meredith claims she had taken our daughter Lily to look, not adopt. Right. Lily has been disqualified as a witness because she was too young to remember. How convenient. I was just numb at this point, busy checking my back pocket to see if, by any chance, my wallet was still with me.

Sam was the most unappealing female I had spent time with since college. There had been that heavyset, funny-looking girl in the sorority up the street from my dorm, but that is another story. It is amazing what hard apple cider will excuse.

Sam was hefty, with muscular legs. The

SAM SHOWING OFF HER DRINKING PROBLEM.

animal was built like a linebacker. She had buckteeth, or was it fangs? Memory is a funny thing. Sometimes you just remember the good stuff. Occasionally I noticed how sharp those instruments of death and destruction were. Sam's jaws did seem particularly powerful.

Plus, there was something foreboding about Sam. After the dog grabbed on to a ball or stuffed animal, usually there was not much left to play with. I would obsess about razor-sharp teeth in my troubled sleep. Truthfully, I was afraid of the animal.

Sam's bark was shockingly robust and very unladylike. Some might even call the throaty eruption threatening. Of course, what can you expect from a female version of Mike Tyson? Do you get the feeling I am leading up to something? Willie had gone to a better place just in time, I figured. Sam would be his warm and cuddly stand-in. Right.

Sam terrorized the neighborhood. People were genuinely afraid of her. Meredith and I routinely receive a lot of Express Mail, FedEx packages, and the like. When delivery trucks roared down the street and timidly ventured onto our driveway, a loud, lumbering lug with a deep bark and bayonets for teeth would take charge of the Welcome Wagon. Reactions came swiftly. No complaints, just raw fear.

The frightened UPS driver traveled part of the way down the driveway, put away any thought of a signature, and heaved packages out his open sliding door before Sam could jump in and eat his leg. Occasionally I would witness the encounter. The look of utter terror on the guy's face was hard to describe, resembling Barbara's in *Night of the Living Dead* when she first confronted a ghoul.

Other companies delivering goods and services simply refused deployment to the war zone known as our property. I watched the mailman age over time, as if he were the president in a time of war. Sam sat on the front steps each day, flexing and waiting, ready to do battle.

There was no way I was going to lock her up indoors. You do not invite a terrorist into your home. We were perplexed, not to say worried. In my mind, we were going to need a legal team to hold on to the property when the lawsuit inevitably came. Miraculously, it never

did. Mer said little, but I thought she seemed weary.

Meredith's former assistant, Amanda, remembers Sam attacking her regularly when she arrived to work at the house. "That dog snarled and tore my clothes before I could make it inside." Amanda moved her family to Tennessee. She claims her husband is in the Navy and was reassigned there. I think I know better.

When the crazy carnivore was kept in the house, unattended and free to roam the interior, anything could happen. Raw steaks left on counters to defrost went missing. Baked goods in bags were reduced to mere crumbs, packaging torn open and left for dead. Nothing edible could be left out, and Sam seemed to have a cast-iron stomach. She could devour anything.

Even Meredith knew we had to do something. That alone was shocking. "I will talk to the dog lady at *The View*," she assured me. I did not know what a dog lady was, maybe half woman and half dog, but I was desperate and ready for anything.

The dog lady introduced us to Mike, a dog trainer with some draconian ideas about whipping errant animals into line. Mike was about to be deployed to Iraq. This guy will do fine, I thought.

"When dogs do something wrong," Mike explained, "you have about one and a half seconds to deal with it. Then they forget what they have done." I have no clue where he got that one, but I told him I thought he was overestimating Sam's intelligence.

Mike brought along a special electric collar, delightfully dangerous and more portable than an electric chair. This was no ordinary electric collar, designed to put out a modest charge to keep dogs on the property. This collar generated enough electricity to drop a cow in its tracks.

One of us (me, I insisted) would handle the remote control unit and do the deed as needed. It will be emotionally wrenching work, I said to Meredith, but one of us has to do it. What I won't do for the community. The idea was to hide the control device and stay at a distance so the dog believed it was God or the Great Pumpkin wearing the executioner's hood.

Here was the plan. When Sam went for the postman's leg or the lamb chops on the kitchen table, her inevitable move for the meat, she would get zapped. "How much voltage can I throw at her?" I asked Mike. I couldn't wait. He shrugged. "Up to you," he answered. "Just bake something and leave it on a table."

I waited outside the back door and watched. It did not take long. As Sam's paws hit the top of the table, the current hit the bottom of her neck. A yelp and Sam fled, cake intact, dog freaked out.

I had a surging sense of power. Years of frustration would burn off when I pressed a button and sent the painful message to the animal: "I am watching." Meredith looked more than troubled. I told the wife I was going to buy her a present, maybe her own electric necklace, if she did not stop stocking our house with psychotic animals. The threat scared her so badly she ignored me.

It was time for the next step, to make our driveway safe for democracy. The delivery people needed to be free from fear. I put a comfortable chair on the front stoop and grabbed a newspaper. After all, a man has got to be informed and keep a lethal weapon hidden from sight.

And along came the FedEx truck, followed by a speeding bullet and a burst of a bark, the yelp heard 'round the world. The predator was dropped in her tracks. The battle was won. Singing munchkins danced around our property.

Sam ignored the music and returned unsteadily to the stoop, tail between her legs. I could get used to this, I thought. If this seems cruel, remember that it saved human legs and probably the dog, which sooner or later would have disappeared into the night if I had anything to do with it. And I would leave no evidence.

All was quiet on the western front for a while. Commerce once again flowered and bloomed on our street. It may have been an uneasy peace, but that has worked in the Middle East for decades.

Then one summer afternoon, our dear friend Anne stopped by on an errand. Anne had been around Sam enough that she paid the dog little attention. Anne just sauntered into the house through the front door. Meredith turned the corner from the living room just in time to witness the dog launch her attack.

Sam sank her teeth into Anne's hand so ferociously that it took a visit to the emergency room and stitches to make Anne whole. If the victim had been a stranger, the calls from lawyers would have come soon enough. Anne was forgiving and left the matter in Meredith's hands.

I was on a train home from New York City when the call came. Meredith was in tears, not only because of Anne's injuries but also because the vet had told her that Sam should be put down. My good wife was undone. When I saw her later that night, I realized it would never happen. A humane doggie demise was not in the cards. Lethal injection is fashionable in Texas, but Meredith would find another solution.

Through our vet, Meredith found a farm in Utah that took in troubled dogs. They were reluctant to take Sam, preferring to work with animals from inside the state, but Meredith put enough money on the table that they thought adopting Sam was a terrific idea. It took a while to make the arrangements. Sam needed to be flown out West. I asked Meredith if Samantha would be flying first class. She ignored the question.

The preparations for the transaction took long enough that the vet prescribed doggie downers to sedate the animal and keep her from chewing up our neighbors. Sam remained in our custody.

Occasionally I slipped an overdose to the dog, though not enough to do her in. I guess I just wanted to imagine what she would look like laid out. Very mature of me. My explanations were at the ready. I don't know, honey, maybe she had a heart attack.

Of course, nothing happened to the killer beast. I think she would have shrugged off cyanide or a lethal injection. Finally, cute little Samantha was crated up and shipped off. Gone. The Liberty Bell tolled that day.

Meredith immediately started talking up the idea of traveling to Utah to visit Sam. I told her I would rather take the short train ride up the river to visit Sing Sing. I said that I saw no reason *ever* to travel to Utah and promised if she did make the pilgrimage, our house would be empty when she returned.

A new sense of well-being was mine for a few months. All was right again. Peace had returned to the house. Meredith cheerfully agreed to lay off the dogs for a while, perhaps a long while. Maybe forever. Her affable demeanor should have been my first clue that we would be going to the dogs again soon. But I chose to believe her.

Foolish, foolish boy. What could I have been thinking? I took Meredith at her word. No matter how often Lucy yanked the ball away at the last second, Charlie Brown did not doubt her and put his all into every kick. Like Charlie, I ended up flat on my back.

I stopped at the kids' school one afternoon, looking for a ride home. There was Amanda, Meredith's trusty assistant at the time. We headed out. I rode shotgun. Gabe and Lily had after-school activities. Ben was in the backseat. Amanda turned to me. "Do you know?" she asked with a straight face. She wore no expression but looked away, pulling out of the school's busy driveway. Silence. Instantly I knew. "Know what?" Ben demanded. Again, silence.

I did not ask the dreaded question, but the answers flowed fast and furious. After school, Meredith had taken Lily into a pet store next to Jasper's, a favored pizza hangout. Later, Gabe joined them. They were in there, Amanda remembers, for what seemed like hours. They took turns holding the adorable puppy. And he *was* adorable. What puppy isn't? A purchase was assured.

Of course, I was furious, not that anybody noticed or cared. Our no-dog treaty had been abrogated. There was little I could do but sulk like a ten-year-old, which made me the youngest one in the family. This would be my Spring of Discontent, but the family did not look up from the new puppy long enough to take note. Spring would melt into summer and all the seasons thereafter.

Over the Edge

Jasper quickly grew from puppy to dog. He looked a little like Willie. Whatever his faults, Willie had been relatively calm, emphasis on *relatively*. Jasper was noise in motion, hands down infinitely more annoying than Willie.

Jasper was a little strung out, probably already on some controlled substance. Even as a puppy, there was a hideous shrillness to his tiny bark. This was when my teeth started to hurt.

The house was up for grabs. Jasper was cast in a supporting role at this point. His moment would come. When it came to destroying family tranquility, Jasper had to wait his turn. The cats had become Public Enemy Number One.

Every dog needs a cat to keep the cartoon moving. This film would become a horror movie. Over the years, we had lost two cats to old age. Now we were blessed with two more, big, inbred New York City street cats that carried loaded weapons and took nothing from anybody. Natural-born killers.

Game on.

Our New York City vet had pawned the

cats off on Meredith, yes, and me when they were kittens. I did not really get a vote, anyway. Surprised? The kids were in on this one, and I was outnumbered.

The vet probably figured we were not bright enough to know that kittens grow into cats. Among her finest qualities, Meredith also is a cat person. I am such a lucky guy. Go ahead and shoot me.

I think cats are horrid animals. There is no cat litter on this earth that can mask what these cats leave behind. But, to make matters worse, the latest citizens of our land became enormous felines, menacing, take-no-prisoners predators. The neighbors were warning their children, locking their doors.

Felipe is jet-black and so large he could

give any jungle animal a run for its money. Felipe is a panther that allows Jasper to clamp his powerful jaws around the empty feline head and drag the two-hundred-pound cat all over the kitchen. They both belong in a traveling circus.

Felipe has such pleasure in his eyes. Excitement. We may have the weirdest sado-masochistic pet shelter in the county. I am quite certain Felipe could eliminate Jasper with one big bite but enjoys his secret pleasures too much. Their relationship has not always been so openly sexual, but their comfort with each other has defied cartoon caricatures.

Felipe's sister, Sweet Pea, is a coconspirator. The smaller cat jumps onto counters with Felipe to tear open loaves of bread and any

SWEET PEA DIGS DIRT FOR FOOD.
NOT TOO BRIGHT.

food they can reach. Once, I brought home a deli sandwich for Ben, securely wrapped and sealed in a bag. I put it on the counter and yelled for Ben to come and get it.

By the time Ben flew down the stairs, the packing lay on the floor in shreds, and the sandwich and cats had vanished. We began storing baked goods and assorted other foods in dish cabinets around the kitchen.

The cats are on the counters, whenever they please and regardless of whether we are around or out of position. They troll for whatever we are careless enough to leave around. One evening we were going to sit and watch the news before dinner.

"Do you want some cheese while you watch the news, Richard?" Meredith yelled out as I headed down the stairs. "Sure," I answered, and walked into the family room where the television sits. Meredith was standing in the adjacent kitchen. There on a table sat an empty cheese plate. A fat cat was missing in action.

As I was writing this sad story, I wandered down to the kitchen one afternoon. The big garbage drawer had been left open a crack. That was all it took. A criminal needs only a small opening to find what he wants.

The garbage was everywhere, spread around the large kitchen floor. Felipe sat nearby paying no attention. I yelled at the top of my lungs. I hissed at the animal. That used to scare him. Felipe remained motionless, appearing bored.

The next morning, the sun had not even

made an appearance when I looked up from the newspaper to see this black panther perched on top of the garbage drawer, which he had casually pulled open. I hissed, this time loudly enough to awaken the neighbors. I might as well have been hissing at the stove.

Felipe just looked at me, making no move to jump down and get away. In the predawn silence, I thought I heard him swear at me. Then he went back to his digging. The scorn on the cat's face gave me pause. Only when I started to get up did he walk—not run, but amble—away. If cats had fingers, it was clear where the middle digit would be pointing. I knew he would be back.

Who lives this way? I demanded. We do, I thought. The cats have figured out how to

Feline.
STALKING A NEIGHBOR.

pull virtually every cabinet open if it is not nailed shut or has no armed guard posted in front of it.

We have lost entire loaves of bread in a single instant. Tell me again, I beseech Meredith desperately. Tell me. Teach me. I need to know. Why do we have these animals? "To enrich our lives," we answer together.

Felipe really does look threatening, like he should be roaming the mountains or guarding a high-security prison. The animal is lithe and large, all muscle with a penchant for bloodshed that any serial killer would admire.

Felipe disappears for days and returns home carrying dead birds, squirrels, rodents, and any formerly living thing he can bury his claws into. They almost always land in the kitchen. I live in fear that I will come home one day to see the animal dragging around a mangled mail carrier or neighbor.

Do you have any idea what it is like to open the back door on a sunny summer morning, inhale deeply, and find a dead animal so mangled it is impossible to identify? How about a fat squirrel without a head? Does anybody else live this way?

Sweet Pea is also fond of bringing all kinds of small animals into the house. These chipmunks, or whatever the little beasties are, come in alive. Sweet Pea is a pacifist. She spends her time batting them around like badminton birdies before releasing them.

Then the fun begins. The race to beat the executioner to his prey is on. Hysterics break out because Meredith and her glass jar have showed up. She is determined to rescue them before Felipe discovers Sweet Pea's captive and seals the deal.

The wretched cats still walk the earth. In fact, they seem to like life at our address. Living with all the animals is so relaxing. One of the cats wanders the halls at night, with the creepy habit of wailing at the top of its lungs, as if he or she is perishing in pain. Meredith could sleep through a nuclear attack. Not me. I am up, wondering if this is the ghost of Christmas past.

My new theory is that the wailing comes from both cats, their collective guilt for torturing and, well, let's say, helping other animals into the big sleep. Certainly it couldn't be that they are crying out of sheer joy, knowing that once again, they are enriching our lives.

In school, facts like these were known as *context*; in our case, they're the backdrop for the ascent of Jasper in our lives. The blessed feline beasts have only been a sideshow for the kids. The dog is the main attraction.

Of course, our children had their own lives, school, soccer, the stage. What did they care? They could fiddle as Rome burned. I was in a different place. Four barking dogs, three French hens, two prowling cats, and a partridge in a pear tree were more than enough for me.

Sam had retired out West, and it really had been time to stop; this time for sure. But there is no stopping my good wife. I do not know why. Meredith still manages to keep a straight face, clinging to her claim that Gabe told her that animals restore joy in families.

The woman has been dining out on that one for years. Of course, there were no witnesses to Gabe's observation. My son is at school in Chicago now, presumably living, well, a colorful college life. He has no recollection of the statement, but the old memory bank may just be overdrawn.

BORN TO BARK

Our menagerie currently resembles an Al Qaeda cell. I fear for the community. Jasper's bark is big now. Bigger than he is. I wish I could describe the horrible noise that passes for a bark. It is an insult to dog dignity, an embarrassment to hardworking four-legged creatures. And this dog barks the way I breathe. Constantly.

I look around, indoors and out. Nothing is

going on. There are no intruders or wild animals in the vicinity, just peace and quiet broken by his arbitrarily spaced barking. Jasper barks for the same reason other male dogs lick their private parts. Because he can.

Jasper was born to bark.

That shrill noise had come close to getting us evicted from a borough of New York City. In 2004, we were set to renovate our house: tear it down and try again. The project would take more than a year. We would be displaced to the Bronx.

Our kids still lived at home and considered themselves prisoners of the suburbs there. We were living in a small village along the Hudson River and owned enough land so Jasper only annoyed the hell out of me, but this move would

JASPER. DOING WHAT HE DOES BEST. NOTHING.

place us in the big time, Big Town. This would be the Big Apple, where no prisoners are taken.

We would be in New York City in the heart of a tough borough. People live on top of one another there. I imagined Jasper would make enemies fast and meet a violent end. Maybe there would be a gangland killing, an end to the dog. Okay, I said. I'm there.

Meredith, inventing her own reality, assured me that the neighbors, though some were living ten feet from us, would have no problem with Jasper. In my mind's eye, I still saw a hit. I mean, this was the Bronx. Da Brawnx. The move went off without a hitch. I waited patiently. It did not take long. The barking started.

The neighbors reacted. The cops came.

To my horror, the police were nice about the barking, even understanding. "That's what dogs do," one said. I cannot say the same about the community reaction, which was less charitable. The kids fielded irate phone calls. Angry passersby came to the door and vented, even to Lily, who was barely twelve at the time. Jasper brings out the best in people.

We lived a half block from a sprawling apartment complex. One day, a petition showed up, stuffed under the front door. The document demanded that we get rid of the animal and was signed by a large group from the apartment house. Finally, Meredith was upset. "What are we going to do?" she asked nervously. "I'm going to sign the petition," I answered.

The protest went nowhere. Their bark was worse than their bite.

Back to cats for a moment: While we were in the Bronx, Beanbag, another cat that enriched our lives (remember Spike, the petrified cat? Beanbag was her brother), gave Gabe a present. We were up at 4:00 a.m. to get Gabe ready for a school field trip to Quebec. Beanbag had slept on Gabe's new parka and confused it with the men's room at the bus station. I don't know about you, but cat urine is one of my favorite aromas.

For lack of a better predawn solution, Meredith sprayed the coat with some awful cleaner and told Gabe to go outside in the freezing darkness and roll in the snow. "That's okay, Mom," Gabe said. "I'm just sitting with

BEANBAG.
In Memoriam. HARMLESS.

the guys." The guys noticed nothing, probably thinking Gabe was wearing some exotic new scent.

Beanbag left the owners of the rental a going-away present. The world's largest urine specimen on a couch. (Wasn't that an Olympic event?) We had to buy a new couch, which enriched our bank account. But we were alive, and so was our marriage. I had hated the year, but at last we were going home. Of course, Jasper went with us.

The kids are gone now. They are happy, and so are we. Sort of. The horrible animal now sleeps on the floor of our bedroom. Ugh. Meredith says she likes having that furry burglar alarm around, especially when she is alone. That is hard to argue *against*, though we never have had a burglar. The dog generally lies around the house, existing, or deterring burglars.

At holiday time, Jasper wears a necklace of jingle bells so the neighbors can tell their children those tinkling bells they hear are Santa Claus in the distance. Hearing the melodious mammal up close is a real treat, though he rarely gets up to move anywhere except, of course, to follow Meredith around or attack me.

It is the damnedest thing. The animal is glued to my wife. Jasper loves Meredith more than dog food itself. He will spend the day outside our room if she is inside and has locked the door (even Meredith has limits), waiting and watching for the opportunity to leap into her arms.

JASPER. AFTER TOO MUCH TO DRINK AT A HOLIDAY PARTY.

Anywhere Meredith goes, upstairs or down, inside or out, the dog trails her. "Whither thou goest, I will go," the Book of Ruth tells us in the Bible, "and where thou lodgest, I will lodge; thy people shall be my people." Wait a minute. Please tell me I am not one of that shrieking dog's people, I imagine saying to the rebbe.

A trainer who once took Jasper for a while answered the desperate question, what's going on here? The guy pronounced Jasper "extremely possessive." Duh. Jasper follows Meredith from room to room, even into the bathroom. Have you no sense of privacy, woman? I demand. I know you feed him, but this is crossing the line. Meredith just looks through me.

When I hear the dog running down the

stairs, it means Meredith is not far behind. The animal is like a Secret Service agent. He functions as a self-appointed bodyguard. When anyone approaches Meredith with open arms, poised to kiss her on the cheek, Jasper snarls and lunges.

If Meredith is lying on the couch or in bed and I move to join her, my jugular is at risk. Meredith simply says, "No, Jasper." That sure makes a difference. The beast is not playing, just guarding his common-law wife. This mean mammal could pose as a Doberman, except when he is hungry. Then we are fraternity brothers, all for one and one for all.

Meredith insists Jasper is a smart dog. I do not think so. The animal cannot name the capital of New York and is content to eat dog food every day. When he behaves, I promise him water with his next meal. If he is very good, I mean exemplary, there is a special treat. Dog food, again.

I have to trick Jasper into going outside, which he never wants to do. I am smarter than the dog is. Not by much, Meredith suggests. I leave a door open and eventually he sees or hears something and goes out. Genius. Jasper will chase anything not nailed down. Not another dog, of course. That would be too much work. And Jasper's little legs would never work that hard. He would demand a lunch break.

No, Jasper is more likely to go after a leaf gently falling from a tree. He repeats the exercise many times an hour. All the while, his shriek can be heard in the next county or picked up by Navy intelligence from a submarine in the Indian Ocean.

Other dogs run and jump and play outdoors. We have a large enough property with an electric fence, heaven for an ordinary dog. Ours whines to get back in minutes after he leaves the house. There is nothing worse than a whining dog. Man up, I yell to deaf ears. If Meredith is there, she jumps to her feet to let the beast back in.

No response to the bark? The dog is so determined to find Mama and stay by her side that he chews through screen doors and throws his ample bulk at the barrier. Jasper is, well, a bit overweight. A large tear in the screen magically appears. The two are reunited.

By Meredith's count, this has happened seven times. The animal breaks through. The door is repaired. That is called perpetual motion. And we are left supporting the local economy.

"Why don't you leave him out and let him pretend he is a dog?" I ask. "You are a broken record," she responds. Jasper prefers sounding off from a corner of the couch in the family room.

This is how smart the smart dog is. He routinely stands in front of our car and bites the license plate as we start to pull out of the driveway. He remains in front of the car as we pick up speed. A slip of the right foot would turn him into a pancake. At the last minute, Jasper steps aside and barks himself silly as we pull away.

Smart.

Jasper's claim to a working brain comes because, after watching us push down on our horizontal door handle for years, he finally has learned to jump on it and use his weight to pop open the front door. The animal seems to be particularly fond of popping the door open on frigid winter days. My study sits directly up the stairs from that door. Instantly there is a sub-zero wind tunnel that I have to deal with.

Going up and down stairs to close doors is hard for me because I have multiple sclerosis and walk with a cane. I move at a glacial pace and see glaciers forming as I head for the door. If that animal is so smart, why doesn't he learn to shut the freaking door behind him? Jasper just sneers as I close the door. He knows I cannot catch him. I am just grateful he doesn't pull the door open as soon as I get back upstairs.

When he's not attacking, the dog makes a show of not just ignoring me, but pretending I do not exist. I can walk by him, though if I get too close, the little darling growls under his breath and shows me his teeth. That is just his gentle gesture of contempt to remind me he is still here.

When Meredith goes away on business, Jasper is beside himself. More than that, he is pissed off and expresses his displeasure by using the living room as his personal bathroom. You can't flush a floor. Meredith calls and I calmly tell her the dog has enriched our lives all over the living room.

We raised three children. Who needs a dog that acts out? You guessed it: Not me.

Meredith has traveled the world and left me alone with the kids. She trusted me, and if she had qualms about passing the baton (mothers usually do), she did not share them. But she does not trust me with Jasper when she leaves town. Meredith routinely checks on the dog's health when she calls.

Always, the same question finds its way into the mix at the end of the conversation: "By the way . . . how is Jasper?" I think she believes she will detect something in my voice if the dog is already suffering from a bad case of rigor mortis.

My wife delights in telling anyone who will listen that Richard hates dogs. I do not hate all dogs. I like other people's animals or those I cannot have. And I do not hate our dog. I hate the word *hate*. I do. *Hate* is imprecise and so overused. I just want Jasper to go away. "Run away, Scar," Simba commands. "And never return." That worked in *The Lion King*.

Our dog, I mean Meredith's dog, can lie peacefully in a comfortable position with a bed of rose petals under his head or in front of a moving dump truck for all I care. That is his choice, and I will defend his right to make it. But I am resigned to a basic reality. Jasper is here to stay.

The dog will continue its annual ritual of scaring cute kids away on Halloween. The dog will keep shrieking at dawn, a special pleasure after a late night. Meredith will keep feeding Jasper leftover steak from the table so he can enrich our lives all over the place overnight. And best of all, Meredith will have to keep asking for Jasper's permission to kiss me goodnight. Unacceptable.

And Jasper will live to bury me.

Dogs are survivors, though according to Thomas Berger's *Little Big Man,* they were a staple in the diet of Native Americans making their way across the Great Plains. I will not even bring up the common assumptions about Chinese restaurants. And yet dogs have wormed their way into American culture. Of course, the dog is ritualistically celebrated by authors in search of books and movie directors looking for surefire winners at the box office.

Forget the silver screen. It is real life that drives me crazy. It snowed last night. That blanket of white is a seasonal constant and reassures me that all is right in my world. Then I open my newspaper and make a cup of coffee. I read about war and politics, but I jump out of my skin when I learn that Pet Airways is in trouble. Pet Airways? What the heck is that?

Guess. No more cargo holds for Phoebe, one lady's ten-year-old miniature schnauzer, according to *The New York Times*. Now, get this. Attendants cater to the animals during the flight, and there is a pet lounge "for the emotional goodbye at the airport." The airline was founded by some California guy. What a surprise. I glance out the window. The snow is gone.

Writer Bruce McCall had it about right. He is sufficiently sick of the animal scene to serve my cup of tea. McCall soothed my spirit in *The New Yorker* with "Pet Books Proliferate," served with a choice of corn syrup or saccharine. McCall told the tragic tale of "Tess, the Orphan Earthworm." "Tess was inside the toaster, napping. Chuck decided to make himself a Pop-Tart. . . . A few hours later, still sobbing, I carried the dangling little question mark of charred gristle that had been my Tess out to the back flower bed."

No sloppy high emotion here. I, for one, could not figure out if this sad story was fiction or a true account of a wonderful worm story. Chuck could not be reached for comment. My comment is that I worry about our culture: that it is in peril and possibly going to the dogs.

Well, I just cannot worship our dog, if you hadn't guessed. If dogs guide us on our journeys, if it takes a beast to show me the way along life's obstacle course, I will end up in the Hudson River. I am a two-time cancer survivor and have battled MS for decades. No dog has eased my pain. I am legally blind and have stepped where I should not have too many times. Wiping off my shoes for the millionth time is not my idea of how I want to live.

I would like to take our animals and box them or put them in a crate marked "Return to Sender." My good wife operates under a different, perhaps more honorable value system that is hard to argue against, and so my wishes go unfulfilled.

"You don't get rid of a member of the family just because they are difficult," I heard her tell a visitor to our house, "or they don't quite work out like you want." Hell. Not just the dogs, but I will be toast if she changes her mind about that.

I have apologized many times in my life. Not this time. For those I have offended, I say, tough nuggies. Jasper gets to sleep indoors and feed his face twice a day. What else do I owe him? I will have no pet pedestal erected on my property. It is only one more place to clean up after Jasper.

Long ago, when my thoughts wandered to

the very idea of owning a dog, I visualized a dignified, lumbering animal by my side. A man's dog, if you will. He would be powerful yet gentle, with a deep bark used sparingly and only when necessary. Above all, the dog would value loyalty and be my friend.

"He guards the sleep of his pauper master as if he were a prince," George G. Vest wrote in his book *Eulogy of the Dog,* published in 1870. A dog lived for the master in those days, right up to the end. "There by his graveside will the noble dog be found, his head between his paws and his eyes sad but open in alert watchfulness, faithful and true, even unto death."

Yup. That's Jasper, a trusted friend and canine companion who will be by my side, even as I go to my grave before he finds his. In floods or fire or famine, my dog will guard my resting place. I know that.

Actually, the beast will relieve himself on my grave, I am pretty certain. His pals Felipe and Sweet Pea will have discovered a new litter box. Eternal humiliation.

I tell myself that life is good and everything works out in the end. Maybe next time, I will have better luck.

Did I say next time?

ACKnowLeDGments

By now it must be evident that Meredith and I find ourselves on different pages in the endless doggie debate. But if this is as bad as it gets in our marriage, screw the dog. Jasper lives, and I will survive the hideous howling until the animal screams his last meaningless mouthful. I mean, how long can the loud loser keep going?

Actually, I do not want to know.

I do want to acknowledge Meredith's long-standing support for this book, though she knew from the get-go that she would cringe at every harsh judgment I would offer. It must have killed her. Meredith is a real friend, a great journalist, and true professional who appreciates the power of story. She does not seem to care what I say about her, which I find mildly insulting. Very Queen Elizabeth.

Before Meredith read the manuscript, I asked my agent if there was anything she had read that might hurt Meredith's feelings. "No," the woman replied thoughtfully. "Meredith comes across as a kind, caring person." And me? I asked. Linda paused. "You come across as an asshole." Good, I quickly replied. My work is done.

Linda Loewenthal is not shy about sharing her opinions. I have the scars to prove it. Linda worked me until the manuscript was ready for a publisher. Linda is a great partner. My editor at Penguin, Vanessa Kehren, never stopped laughing as she ran a tight ship, getting the book ready for publication. My thanks also go to David Rosenthal, president of Blue Rider Press, his imprint at Penguin, for instantly seeing this book's potential. Aileen Boyle, David's associate publisher, is a publicity and marketing wizard. Only she could sell a book about doing in a dog. Stan Mack's illustrations bring my story to life. Stan is fun, which made our collaboration even better.

Last, I want to thank Jasper for his never-ending sense of humor. I told the dog about the book, and he went for my throat. As Bugs Bunny once laughed scornfully, "What a maroon."

About the Author

Richard M. Cohen is the author of two *New York Times* bestsellers: a memoir, *Blindsided: Lifting a Life Above Illness,* detailing his struggles with MS and cancer and his controversial career in the news business, and *Strong at the Broken Places: Voices of Illness, a Chorus of Hope,* chronicling the lives of five individuals living with serious chronic illnesses. His distinguished career in network news earned him numerous awards, including three Emmys and a Peabody. Cohen lives outside New York City with his wife, Meredith Vieira. They have three grown children.